THE DANGEROUS BOOK OF POETRY FOR PLANES

Mark Yakich

THE DANGEROUS BOOK OF POETRY FOR PLANES

👓 EYEWEAR PUBLISHING

First published in 2017
by Eyewear Publishing Ltd
Suite 333, 19-21 Crawford Street
Marylebone, London w1h 1pj
United Kingdom

Cover design and typeset by Edwin Smet
Printed in England by TJ International Ltd, Padstow, Cornwall

isbn 978-1-911335-38-2

*Eyewear wishes to thank Jonathan Wonham for his
generous patronage of our press.*

Bowdlerised by Dr Swift.

WWW.EYEWEARPUBLISHING.COM

The Wright Brothers created the single greatest
cultural force since the invention of writing.
– Bill Gates

The odds of a plane crash are normally
1 in 5 million on a commercial carrier.
– Fear of Flying app 'Am I Going Down?'

TABLE OF CONTENTS

MILE HIGH WOMAN

AIRPLANE, INSIDE THE SAFE

Looking down
At puff-pastry clouds

From a porthole window,
Utterly still yet traveling more

Than five hundred miles per hour,
Warm, calm, and contemplating a misdemeanor

In the back of the plane – who would it harm
To beat off one of these men?

As compared to riding in an automobile
Wilbur Wright called flying 'real

Poetry.' One cannot be sure of his sex
Life, but he seems to have been complex

Enough never to marry
Or make love in a lavatory

During violent turbulence.
It's poetry or it's

Novel. Either way flying wears
Me out, not unlike the years

I've spent watching naughty wives
Or husbands with perfect lives

Walk down the center aisle.
I keep wishing that one day while

Some man is ogling my very blond hair,
He'll die right there in the air.

BACKRUB, REQUEST FOR

Against the seatback pocket
I know a lot

Of people like myself
Who like my self

Sometimes.
But it's asinine

To grow
Love affairs out of exit row

Stares. If the man next to me
Reads trashy

Fiction, it's not right
To suddenly put my hand on his thigh.

I could use porn
To sublimate being alone,

But for night terrors
Nothing mollifies. One must bear

The universe's multifarious
Mathematics.

$1 + 1 = 2$. Of course.
And $1 + 1 = 1$. À la sex.

But who can forget lying
Stick-still in bed, after arguing

About having kids – there's no question –
I + I = II.

CELEBRITY, THE GREATEST OF ARTS IS THE ART OF

Charles Lindbergh wasn't the first to fly the Atlantic.
He was the sixty-seventh.

But he was the first to fly it solo.
That is, two heroes aren't as interesting as one.

Some religions insist that there aren't multiple gods, only
One god. And that religion called technology

Is no different. In parlance,
It's a 'cure' – not 'cures' – for cancer.

Yet here's Lindbergh in an interview shortly before he died,
'I realized that if I had to choose, I

Would rather have birds than airplanes.' I'm not
The first to point it out, but I probably point

It out more than most: A plane overhead
Looks more like a flying cross than it does a bird.

Jesus wasn't the only one crucified on Passover;
But He's the One we remember.

ECCLESIASTES, WORKING TOWARD

I am here in the middle
Of reading a terrible

Book that claims looking through a telescope
Is more sensible than being up

In a plane at 34,000 feet,
Sputtering retreats.

The telescope sits on top of a mountain,
And all the scientists are certain

That the observatory is not just a pimple
On the back of a turtle.

I am here in the middle
Of reading a brilliant

Book on a plane, but then
The wings begin

Waving at me. I'm frightened
And then embarrassed.

I look down and feel
Like a weed

A wind slips through.
Suddenly a hand slips through

My hair, and I don't mind it's not
My husband's. Trouble is, the guilt

I don't feel but know should be there,
The light of a dead star.

FAMILY, RECOVERING

Back in Coos Bay for Thanksgiving
Dinner, it doesn't matter which one of them brings

The drama. Half a dozen
Fight for center stage. As for the two, single, middle-aged cousins,

They'll probably fillet each other
With cranberry-stained ring fingers, sometime later.

And given the chance, the teenage girls would beat off
The boys who, on the whole, aren't worth

That bottle of salad dressing. They lie all evening
Long on Grandmom's divan wondering

Which one of them has the longest penis.
Innocuous talk, Mom says, *a passing virus*.

You consider climbing out the bathroom window,
But are foiled in the hallway by an in-law.

At the dining room table everyone cups their
Hands, waiting for Granddad to begin the prayer.

But all you can think about is who
Your ex-boyfriend used to sit next to.

When thanks are done and everyone is
Seated, stand back up. Close

Those eyes. They think they know you.
You think you know you. You know nothing and no one.

Let the curse-filled tears begin.
It's time to prove your multitudes hold meaning.

MAKE-OUT, INFINITE

The brain
Can't feel a thing.

How could it –
Gaze out at that

Cumulonimbus.
It's so fucking gorgeous,

Sometimes the pilot wants to lose
The plane in it. Yes, the brain does

Lie in the sky – Miss Emily
Dickinson knew it without flying.

And were she here now
With me, somehow

I'd take her hand and say,
Mother, you've always

Been my only sun.
And I wouldn't even dream

Of setting my lips on her clavicle.
It'd be ineffable

Enough to run a finger
Over her prayer

Beads while she draws the endless
Sky into her hymnal.

READER, THE AIRPLANE

I'm most aware of another's countenance
When I'm on a plane.

Because the thought of something
Going wrong runs through my mind

Every other thought, I feel I must memorize
The faces of my fellow pilgrims.

It's an act of contrition
For ignoring humans

For too long – likely
Since the last time I

Flew. The standard thought:
At some catastrophic moment

I shall be forced to clutch the midriff
Of the person barfing

Next to me. If he's a good-looking
Man, it's a comforting

Thought. But then my mind turns to disgust
At my bias against

Homeliness. When the end is near, friend,
Take me from behind

As if you're trying to smash a window
With an airplane pillow.

SEX, PHILANTHROPIC

There's still plenty of life left
In this wannabe widow, so let's get on with

The paid performance. You don
Your trouser hard-on,

And I'll wear your wife's favorite
Black dress. Then we'll celebrate –

For getting the bereavement
Fare was an achievement

She would have been proud of.
But if you say *I love*

You, I'll knock out
All your teeth, those chits I'm about

To lick tenderly yet not adore.
Breathing against your

Torso, I'll be Ms. No Problem –
A spent vial of truth serum –

And won't need to be healed
Like a girl by her daddy's

Kiss. Simply admit it:
You've never been jacked off by a hermaphrodite.

I'm going to fuck you and love
You at the same time – let's hope it's enough.

WAY, ON THIS PLANE ALL FACE THE SAME

And yet we shouldn't just sit
There and beat up a silver bag of peanuts

Because we don't want
To use our teeth on it.

If we're willing to die some,
Perhaps heroin

Can restart our lives. But
To sob hard out of earshot

Of a beloved – what's the point?
Life's a transmogrifying thought

Inside the soft and long
Body of death. Who knows

What I or anyone else
Means? Let's stop cutting ourselves

On metaphor alone.
If one could only fuck the person

In one's diary…well, let's ask the air waiter
(That otiose, beautiful stranger).

See if he thinks moaning helps the experience
Of pain. If he quotes

The lion in *The Wizard of Oz*,
Tell him about your layover with gastric lavage.

If he quotes The Bible, remind him
That on the last day of Creation –

The ancient translators were inept –
God didn't rest, He wept.

EXPERIMENTS WITH AIR

YO
U
CANNO
TMA
STUR
BATETOTHISSK
YLINEEACH
MOR
NINGWI
THO
UTEVE
NTUA
LLY
BEI
NGPU
NISH
E
D

MANHATTAN

HORS
EINT
RUCK

BIRD
INPL
ANE

JAC
KIN
JILL

L   Y
RIC
ISM

ONLYWHENAMANCRIESISITCALLEDMAKE-UP
ONLYWHENAMANCRIESISITCALLEDMAKE-UP
ONLYWHENAMANCRIESISITCALLEDMAKE-UP
ONLYWHENAMANCRIESISITCALLEDMAKE-UP
ONLYWHENAMANCRIESISITCALLEDMAKE-UP
ONLYWHENAMANCRIESISITCALLEDMAKE-UP
ONLYWHENAMANCRIESISITCALLEDMAKE-UP
ONLYWHENAMANCRIESISITCALLEDMAKE-UP
ONLYWHENAMANCRIESISITCALLEDMAKE-UP
ONLYWHENAMANCRIESISITCALLEDMAKE-UP
ONLYWHENAMANCRIESISITCALLEDMAKE-UP
ONLYWHENAMANCRIESISITCALLEDMAKE-UP

JURYBOX

PROUDTOBEANAMERICAN
PROUDTOBEANAMERICAN
PROUDTOBEANAMERICAN
PROUDTOBEANAMERICAN
PROUDTOBEANAMERICAN
PROUDTOBEANAMERICAN
PROUDTOBEANAMERICAN
PROUDTOBEANAMERICAN
PROUDTOBEANAMERICAN
PROUDTOBEANAMERICAN
PROUDTOBEANAMERICAN
PROUDTOBEANAMERICAN
PROUDTOBEANAMERICAN
PROUDTOBEANAMERICAN
PROUDTOBEANAMERICAN
PROUDTOBEANAMERICAN

PROUDTOBEANAMERICAN   PROUDTOBEANAMERICAN   PROUDTOBEANAMERICAN
PROUDTOBEANAMERICAN   PROUDTOBEANAMERICAN   PROUDTOBEANAMERICAN
PROUDTOBEANAMERICAN   PROUDTOBEANAMERICAN   PROUDTOBEANAMERICAN
PROUDTOBEANAMERICAN   PROUDTOBEANAMERICAN   PROUDTOBEANAMERICAN
PROUDTOBEANAMERICAN   PROUDTOBEANAMERICAN   PROUDTOBEANAMERICAN
PROUDTOBEANAMERICAN   PROUDTOBEANAMERICAN   PROUDTOBEANAMERICAN
PROUDTOBEANAMERICAN   PROUDTOBEANAMERICAN   PROUDTOBEANAMERICAN
PROUDTOBEANAMERICAN   PROUDTOBEANAMERICAN   PROUDTOBEANAMERICAN
PROUDTOBEANAMERICAN   PROUDTOBEANAMERICAN   PROUDTOBEANAMERICAN
PROUDTOBEANAMERICAN   PROUDTOBEANAMERICAN   PROUDTOBEANAMERICAN
PROUDTOBEANAMERICAN   PROUDTOBEANAMERICAN   PROUDTOBEANAMERICAN
PROUDTOBEANAMERICAN   PROUDTOBEANAMERICAN   PROUDTOBEANAMERICAN
PROUDTOBEANAMERICAN   PROUDTOBEANAMERICAN   PROUDTOBEANAMERICAN
PROUDTOBEANAMERICAN   PROUDTOBEANAMERICAN   PROUDTOBEANAMERICAN
PROUDTOBEANAMERICAN   PROUDTOBEANAMERICAN   PROUDTOBEANAMERICAN
PROUDTOBEANAMERICAN   PROUDTOBEANAMERICAN   PROUDTOBEANAMERICAN

PROUDTOBEANAMERICAN
PROUDTOBEANAMERICAN
PROUDTOBEANAMERICAN
PROUDTOBEANAMERICAN
PROUDTOBEANAMERICAN
PROUDTOBEANAMERICAN
PROUDTOBEANAMERICAN
PROUDTOBEANAMERICAN
PROUDTOBEANAMERICAN
PROUDTOBEANAMERICAN
PROUDTOBEANAMERICAN
PROUDTOBEANAMERICAN
PROUDTOBEANAMERICAN
PROUDTOBEANAMERICAN

PROUDTOBEANAMERICAN
PROUDTOBEANAMERICAN
PROUDTOBEANAMERICAN
PROUDTOBEANAMERICAN
PROUDTOBEANAMERICAN
PROUDTOBEANAMERICAN
PROUDTOBEANAMERICAN
PROUDTOBEANAMERICAN
PROUDTOBEANAMERICAN
PROUDTOBEANAMERICAN
PROUDTOBEANAMERICAN
PROUDTOBEANAMERICAN
PROUDTOBEANAMERICAN
PROUDTOBEANAMERICAN
PROUDTOBEANAMERICAN

MADEINCHINA

```
I
I
IF
IFYOU
IFYOUWANT                               W
IFYOUWANTTOBE                           W
IFYOUWANTTOBEFREE                       WR
IFYOUWANTTOBEFREE                    WRITE
IFYOUWANTTOBE                     WRITEWRIT
IFYOUWANTTO                    WRITEWRITEWRI
IFYOUWANT                  WRITEWRITEWRITEWR
IFYOUWAN                   WRITEWRITEWRITEWR
IFYOUWANTT                    WRITEWRITEWRI
IFYOUWANTTOBE                  WRITEWRITEW
IFYOUWANTTOBEFREE              WRITEWRIT
IFYOUWANTTOBE                   WRITEWRI
IFYOUWANT                     WRITEWRITE
IFYOU                      WRITEWRITEWRI
IF                     WRITEWRITEWRITEWR
I                          WRITEWRITEWRI
                            WRITEWRIT
                               WRITE
                                WR
                                 W
```

ONELONESEATBACK

ISITPOSSI
BLETOWRI
TEALLTHE
REISTOWR
ITEINONES
ENTENCE?

YESANDNO.

PLEA-

SE TAKE

THAT SUN OUT OF

THE

CORNER OF THE SKY

I'D LIKE TO WRITE

MY NAME THERE

AND

SOME-

DAY

GROW FLOW-

ERS

NO-

BODY'S

EVER

SEEN

BE-

FOR

E

ARSPOETICA

```
P E N P A P E R            R
O C C A S I O N A L        L
T   E       A   R          S
Y O U R T R A G I C        C
H         O     P          E
T O B E C O M E            D
A B E L O V E              D
P         O     E          T
S H O U L D N O T          T
H       A     N            G
O       N     A            N
E P I G R A M              M

C A L L M O M              M
A N D D A D                D



          S   O   N   N   E   T
```

BLOOD CHIT MAN

In case they are shot down, military pilots and crew carry 'blood chits', small cards asking foreign civilians for assistance. The U.S. government promises to compensate anyone who helps an American service member to survive, evade, resist, or escape hostile territory and to return to friendly control.

— *Publication 3-50.3 (classified appendix G)*
  Blood Chit Program, U.S. Dept. of Defense

★ I do not speak your language ★ They have instructed me to tell you this first ★ Worldly I am ★ And though digital translators may come across baldly ★ let us not fight over franks and beans and myrrh ★ I am not the virus the last remaining communist designed ★ to put the belch back into the blowjob or to transform the martyr back into Mr. Arty ★ I am not the great argument against exporting the Wonderbra ★ I am not the anti-vagina that is not the penis ★ I am not the whiskers of the broom that can be hand-harvested ★ mop-mistaken ★ or wood-chipped ★ I am not the crack Mama claimed to have found in the cereal box ★ I am not the condom the President lost inside his Secretary of State ★ But I am going to go on and on until you turn me in ★ to your new chief of police ★

★ From above I saw tens of thousands of boys and girls eating freeze-dried potatoes with tiny sticks ★ They reminded me of the hordes of men who poured into Alaska to build a pipeline and often worked eighteen-hour days ★ It was grueling ★ but they got free steak and lobster every night! ★ It's simply one of those things I get melancholic about for no particular reason ★ Like the escalator in the mall that reminds me of when I waited for the bus ★ I was sorry for Mama because she didn't have a car ★ I was sorrier for Papa because he didn't have a job ★ I regretted I'd spent the money they'd given me not on a book but on a Chinese tea set made in Indonesia ★ I didn't even like tea ★ but the cups and saucers were so cute and the book was easier to shoplift ★ Now comes the turn away from the thousands I saw on TV ★ I have nowhere to go back to ★ so there's no point in going on ★ Scratch that ★ I have no time to fuck around with near rhyme ★ On my headstone write ★ whoever thought a ghost could be portrayed with a sheet was an idiot ★

★ Great suffering and weeping are characterized ★ by the orbicularis palpebrarum inferiori ★ and a lot of other unsightly words ★ which draw back the upper part of the cheek and lower lids ★ Therefore my eyes appear closed ★ almost all the time ★ and near their corners ray-like wrinkles form ★ as happens in violent laughter (see Fig. 16a) ★ Also ★ wrinkles form near the root of my nose (Fig. 16b) ★ Secondary signs of suffering and weeping are redness of the whole face ★ which takes in the indigenous ★ down to the letter ★ in places in my body that I am loathe to bare ★ In extreme suffering ★ nervous exhaustion may occur ★ puking and fainting ★ together with partial or total paralysis of my sphincter and anus ★ Much I admit to you ★ has been lost through my anus ★ and that is no joke ★

★ Please take me to someone who will provide for my well-being ★ because a sniper just took out my co-pilot ★ True ★ I didn't like him very much ★ True too ★ It was a beautiful demonstration of pink mist ★ But I promise you that we're all 99.9% genetically the same ★ including the six percent Neanderthal DNA ★ They say we're mere footsteps in footnotes ★ located somewhere between an ape's hatred of his ex-mate ★ and a baby's love of his knitted mittens ★ Shylock said it best ★ we all breed to bleed ★ But Shylock also wanted a pound of flesh ★ It's this difference that creates interest ★ And interest is our pistol and ball ★

★ Broadcasting rules dictate that you won't see my dead body ★ not the right leg coddling the face ★ not the left eye slung-shot from the head ★ lying like a squashed date in the sand ★ If you lose an eye ★ you lose only one fifth of your vision but all of your sense of death ★ I mean depth ★ Fuck it ★ The goddamn medivac never drives fast enough ★ And the flak jacket only attracts attention ★ That's what my wife said the last time we talked ★ So for god's sake don't wear it ★ Well it wasn't anybody's fault I wasn't on TV ★ The ten pints of blood took twenty minutes to leave me ★ No one can hold a selfie that long ★

★ My jaw's broken ★ My skull holds three bullets ★ My buddy keeps one of my toenails because it got blown into his cheek ★ And nobody seems to mind that I wear a wife's garter around my testes ★ I have nothing to do but lay here and look ★ out at that desert there ★ It's like a pasture ★ part past and part future ★ there's no present that's not in the looking ★ or the looking after ★

★ I don't want to die now and then read ★ about it in the morning papers ★ I don't want to write now and have to do a rewrite later ★ I admire the editor of *Stars & Stripes* ★ and would spit into my camo skivvies to prove it ★ Which reminds me that I'm sorry for my heavy bleeding ★ on the carpet of the Queen of England ★ I didn't know it was burgundy and blood wouldn't show up ★ I would like to draw a coward on a piece of paper and then crumple it ★ I would like to delay rush hour on London Bridge ★ by stuffing that crumpled ball into my mouth ★ like the apple in the pig ★ until everybody begs for a slice of my ham ★ And in the slice you happen to get ★ I would like you to carve the paragraph from which I will never escape ★

★ If I'd had a daughter ★ I'd have written you another kind of love letter ★ I'd have popped the dialogue balloon to find out if it truly was filled with poison gas ★ I'd have gone to law school or become a chef ★ I'd have crossed the street at the next light! ★ (Less is happening in my mind but vicariously this time) ★ I'd have eaten the sky and stuck my finger in the moon's caboose ★ just to prove it doesn't smell like cheese ★ In the shady palm of missed chances ★ to lose a thought is to gain a bit of relief ★ The first mouse gets killed ★ the second gets to nibble on the cheddar ★ Do you feel more relaxed now that I'm grounded? ★ I imagine you ★ with your bottomless ass and three locked doors ★ The tiny but loving home of your mind ★ and this day too much kite for its string ★ the clouds are unmoved ★ Yet here we are watching ★ a bride in the town square who succumbs gently to a broom handle ★ I can see her love ★ her death ★ they're about to meet the same fate ★ Angels who only pretend to take directions ★

★ My country will reward you with words that create new worlds ★ and then claim to break hearts into more hearts ★ But it's a mistake ★ Like a pimp with his pride of whores ★ we assume the pimp is a man ★ What's more famous ★ Picasso's 'Guernica' or the little city itself? ★ Although it's true that flying is one of the great universal dreams ★ what if the pilot and first officer fall in love ★ and then forget to put on the autopilot before the rubber? ★ For example the unconscious ★ isn't what Freud thought he'd spend his life recuperating from ★ (If your mama's a whore hurray for your memoir!) ★ As long as the plane is in the air everything is okay ★ As long as we don't pose the hard questions ★ who screwed the guy in the eye? ★ who juiced the electric chair? ★ Every breath doubles as prayer ★

★ One of the reasons you read is to feel ★ connected to a stranger ★ It's flat-out invigorating ★ And so if I'd been killed by blowing myself up with a homemade bomb in Najaf ★ Iraq ★ 21 December 2004 ★ then you would know me but not know me well ★ If I'd been killed when a suicide bomber detonated an explosive inside the mess hall at Camp Marez in Najaf ★ Iraq ★ 21 December 2004 ★ you would love me but not love me well ★ The trick about feeling connected to a stranger besides ★ the person you were as a child or the person you were five years ago ★ or the person you were before reading this ★ is that tricks aren't always tricks ★ It's easy to say for example ★ I was tricked into believing that he loved me ★ that the war was going to be good for humanity ★ that bicycling to work is actually more dangerous than driving ★ But it's not easy to say that you have tricked yourself ★ into believing in other people for the sole reason ★ that there's no choice but to believe in other people ★ The fact is ★ when you're eating a half-destroyed ready-to-eat meal ★ hanging from a half-destroyed tree ★ you'll need someone to help you get down ★ If there's one thing left to be said about the reasons ★ for reading a book ★ it's that too many things go unsaid ★ Do not be misled ★ many people have duped you into thinking you have nothing to say for yourself ★ If you really want to feel connected to some other person ★ you'll stop reading and find a stranger and tell her that it's going to be okay ★ even if it won't be okay ★ and that you love her even if a lot of the time you don't ★ If nothing else ★ you have to believe in the words I love you ★ even if the idea behind them is only ★ Don't forget me after I die ★ The words we have made for ourselves may help ★ you through the dark times ★ but the dark times may not help ★ you through the fields of words where battles never happened ★

★ Growing up ★ killing a chicken for dinner always prompted a quarrel ★ about who had to do it ★ Mama or Papa ★ So what if today folks in my country take tours of virtual slave ships ★ many are drawn to the dead on their holidays ★ For its abundance ★ a large section of Birkenau was named Canada ★ You could get good boots there and sometimes ★ a silk shawl or a jar of pickled herring ★ But it was in America that fake birds were first made ★ to attract native fowl ★ The most familiar kinds of camouflage make one thing appear to be two ★ two things one and so on ★ Camouflage artists make it a tough task to see a figure ★ on a ground (blending) or to distinguish one category of object from another (mimicry) ★ Less familiar but far more effective is dazzle camouflage ★ in which a single thing appears to be a hodgepodge of disparate components ★ At Shakespeare's Globe the actors say ★ the audience always pays better attention ★ when it's raining ★ Mama loved the sun ★ she said ★ because its rays felt like ink to her fingers ★ Mama ★ Honestly I've always found that writing ★ a suicide note is counterproductive ★ If you plan on dying by your own hand ★ don't use pills ★ Swallowing is simply another way of marking time ★

REAL POETRY

Ninety-five percent of airplane crashes have survivors.

#

In March 1910, Houdini became the first person to fly an airplane in Australia. He learned to drive a car in order to help him pilot the plane. After his successful first and only flight, he left Australia never to fly or drive again.

#

According to the 'Arbitron Airport Advertising Study: Exploring an Undiscovered Upscale Medium,' ninety percent of airline magazine readers say they trust what they read in the in-flight publication. Seventy-one percent of airline magazine readers agree (strongly or somewhat) that because they are on a plane, they read the in-flight magazine more closely than magazines they pick up at other locations. Forty-one percent frequently look at the flight route map.

#

The writer Sherman Alexie is fond of saying that in order to avoid crashing, he listens to a mixtape with songs by musicians who died in plane crashes. His logic
is that he doesn't think God would be as ironic as to crash the plane he's flying in as he's listening to the tape.

#

You can do a flyover tour of Antarctica, the world's
last great wilderness, for as little as $1,000. Antarctica
Sightseeing Flights, which operates in conjunction with
Qantas, will take you on a twelve-hour journey, flying as
low as 2,000 feet over the highest parts of the continent.

#

On any given day, more than 87,000 flights are in the
skies in the United States. So says NATCA, the National
Air Traffic Controllers Association. To put this is
tangible terms, NATCA provides a visual: 'It would
take approximately 7,300 airport terminal monitors to
show all the flights controllers handle in a single day
and approximately 460 monitors to show the number of
flights being handled at any one time.'

#

'And if man were to learn to fly — woe, to what heights
would his rapaciousness reach?' wrote Nietzsche in *Thus
Spoke Zarathustra* in 1885.

#

Nobody who did it ever forgets the experience of flying
into Hong Kong's old airport (Kai Tak, 1925-1998): You
flew so low and close to buildings that you could see
TVs flicker inside apartments. Plans for the old airport
keep changing but have included turning it into a cruise
line terminal, a giant stadium, a line of hotels, or a green
space larger than Central Park.

#

'Compared with the motion of a jolting automobile is not flying real poetry?' wrote Wilbur Wright in a letter in 1905.

#

Adjacent to Stockholm's airport is a 747-200 (built in 1976) that's been converted into a hostel. With 25 rooms, 85 beds, and one luxury suite in the cockpit, guests can listen to red-eyes and cargo flights throughout the night. According to the hostel's owners, 'You can hardly stay closer to the air traffic...Perfect for anyone catching an early flight...Now you can easily book a night at Jumbo Hostel prior to your departure for an extraordinary beginning of your trip – as well as stress reduction.'

#

The first emergency safety cards are from the 1920s and are for flights over the English Channel; they contain no images or illustrations, only text, which essentially says that in the event of an emergency passengers should ask the crew for help. In the late 1940s, emergency cards included bits of light humor to mollify fearful flyers, with slogans such as 'Life vests are fashionable and quite handsomely tailored.'

#

Mr. Carl Reese, former flight attendant and 'King of the Safety Card,' has amassed the world's largest collection of safety cards: 70,000.

#

The sculpture 'Mustang,' controversial for its blood-red, demon-like eyes, sits out front of the Denver Airport. It was designed and partially constructed by the artist Luis Jiménez. We must say 'partially,' because Jiménez died while working on the sculpture – the giant horse toppled and crushed him, and the work had to be completed by his wife and sons.

#

The Princess Juliana International Airport on the island of St. Martin is famous for its short runway (7,980 feet), which is just long enough for jumbo jets (747s) to land. Incoming planes pass 30 to 60 feet over the heads of tourists relaxing on Maho Beach.

#

Of the U.S. passenger carriers, only Delta and United still use 747s. The 747 weighs almost a million pounds on take-off. About one third is fuel and less than one tenth is passengers and cargo. Of the six million parts of a 747, three million are rivets.

#

Some 27,000 miles of toilet paper is used at Pittsburgh International Airport in a year – more than enough to circle Earth's equator.

#

Kamikaze comes from 'kami' (divine) and 'kaze' (wind), and was first used in reference to the typhoon that saved Japan from an invading Mongolian fleet in 1281. For four years, the Mongols had been waiting off the coast of Japan in 800 boats. On the night before they were finally to invade Japan, a typhoon ripped the fleet apart. To celebrate, the Japanese held an eleven-day literary festival. In 1944, the Japanese recast kamikaze as planes loaded with explosives piloted by suicides. A few years later, in America, vodka replaced tequila in a margarita and it was called a kamikaze.

#

In 1793, George Washington gave the world's first 'blood chit' to Jean-Pierre Blanchard, a French aeronaut, before he launched the first balloon in North America. The blood chit was a message, written in English because Blanchard spoke none, to whomever might find Blanchard when his balloon came back to earth. From Philadelphia, Blanchard sailed into the sky and eventually landed in Deptford Township, New Jersey. A couple of farmers came upon this alien, and after an offer of a slug from a bottle of wine and some unfolding of a piece of paper, helped Blanchard return to Philadelphia. The wine was probably the better 'sign of friendship and conciliation,' wrote Blanchard in his journal of the event, because only one of the farmers was literate.

#

Isaac Asimov (1920-1992) was not only a master science fiction writer, but also a serious aerophobe. He flew twice in his entire life.

#

The turbine engine (the jet engine) evolved relatively quickly and necessarily as aircraft makers sought higher speeds, greater fuel efficiency, and improved thrust to weight ratios. Today, the typical, high performance turbine airplane engine may have taken twenty years to develop from conception to final product. In the initial planning stages only seventy-five percent of the needed technology would have been available – the other twenty-five percent projected to occur as 'scheduled invention' during the course of the project.

#

'Jesus bolt' is military jargon for the single part of an aircraft that heroically holds the whole contraption together.

#

On July 2, 1982, Lawrence Richard Walters, a thirty-three-year-old truck driver, better known as Lawnchair Larry, took flight in a lawnchair tied to 45 helium-filled weather balloons from San Pedro, California. He rose to 16,000 feet, shot some of the balloons with a pellet gun, and eventually crashed-landed his chair in Long Beach, knocking out power lines and causing a twenty-minute blackout. About his flight, Larry said, 'It was something I had to do. I had this dream for twenty years, and if I hadn't done it, I think I would have ended up in the funny farm. I didn't think that by fulfilling my goal in life – my dream – that I would create such a stir and make people laugh.' After working briefly as a motivational speaker, doing a Timex watch ad, and

appearing on late night TV talk shows, Larry hiked into
the Angeles National Forest one day in 1993 and shot
himself in the heart and died.

#

Neither Orville nor Wilbur Wright ever married.

#

Gershwin's 'Rhapsody in Blue' (1924) is arguably the
best known airline music ever. United Airlines originally
licensed the tune from the Gershwin estate in 1976
for $500,000. Of the piece, Leonard Bernstein wrote:
'[It] is not a composition at all. It's a string of separate
paragraphs stuck together. The themes are terrific —
inspired, God-given. I don't think there has been such an
inspired melodist on this earth since Tchaikovsky. But if
you want to speak of a composer, that's another matter.
Your 'Rhapsody in Blue' is not a real composition in the
sense that whatever happens in it must seem inevitable.
You can cut parts of it without affecting the whole. You
can remove any of these stuck-together sections and the
piece still goes on as bravely as before. It can be a five-
minute piece or a twelve-minute piece. And in fact, all
these things are being done to it every day. And it's still
the 'Rhapsody in Blue.''

#

Amelia Earhart and her co-pilot, Fred Noonan, were lost
at sea on July 2, 1937, somewhere between New Guinea
and Howland Island in the South Pacific. For a number
of years after Amelia's presumed death, her mother lived

on and off in Berkeley, California. According to legend, every evening at sunset she would stand on her balcony overlooking the university's campus and peer out into the San Francisco Bay, hoping to spot her daughter's plane coming in over the water.

#

According to the International Society of Women Airline Pilots, the percentage of women airline pilots is about 5% worldwide (2009).

#

On the first commercial flights, the co-pilot would hand out the in-flight meals (sack lunches). When stewardesses were introduced, they were registered nurses. And later when they were not required to be nurses, many airlines modeled stewardess uniforms after nurse uniforms. (Eastern Airlines bought the uniforms but didn't hire the nurses.)

#

Aviation pioneer Alberto Santos Dumont didn't invent the wristwatch (Patek Philippe did), but before Dumont only women wore wristwatches (as ornaments) and men carried pocket watches. After having to continually look down at his pocket watch during dirigible flights and fumbling with tangled chain and clasp, Dumont finally asked his friend Louis Cartier if he could find a solution. Cartier fashioned a leather strap and buckle to hold the watch in place. Time was never the same.

#

No U.S. carrier flies to Africa, nonstop or otherwise.

#

In 1962, the Nashville Public Library opened a reading room in the municipal airport. It wasn't technically a branch since books couldn't be checked out, only read in the room. Other than a photo from a library calendar with the caption 'Airport Reading Room: 1962-69,' there is little information about the space. In fact, the airport wing where the room was housed no longer exists, and there's no archival mention about its demise.

#

On October 16, 1956, Pan Am Flight 943, 'Clipper Sovereign of the Skies', left Hawaii for San Francisco. Around three a.m. at 21,000 feet, the plane lost two of its four engines. Pilots calculated that they couldn't make it back to Honolulu or push on to California. Fortunately, there was a U.S. Coast Guard cutter, which was serving as an ocean station between Hawaii and California, within a half hour's flying. After emergency preparations, hours of circling, and a dry run at landing, the plane water-ditched near the ship at about eight a.m. All crew and passengers were saved, but the plane and 44 cases of live canaries in its cargo hold sunk to the bottom of the ocean.

#

Two or three seconds after TWA Flight 800 exploded in flight, the nose section broke off completely. The rest of the plane kept on flying for about 40 seconds before it lost all lift.

#

The term 'ambient music' was coined by Brian Eno in his liner notes to his 1978 album *Ambient 1: Music for Airports*. The story goes that Eno conceived of the album after being stuck for several hours in an airport in Germany and being annoyed at what he heard (or did not hear) in the airport. 'Ambient music,' he wrote, 'must be able to accommodate many levels of listening without enforcing one in particular; it must be as ignorable as it is interesting.'

ACKNOWLEDGMENTS

Thank you to the following magazines in which some of these poems previously appeared, sometimes in altered states: *Anti-Poetry, Barnstorm, Columbia Poetry Review, Copper Nickel, Court Green, Exile Quarterly, Guernica, The Laurel Review, nth position, Octopus Magazine, Ovenbird, Omniverse, Paperbag Magazine* and *Prelude*. A variation of 'Real Poetry', co-authored with Christopher Schaberg, appeared in *The Offending Adam*.

MARK YAKICH
is Professor of English at Loyola
University New Orleans, Editor of *New
Orleans Review*, and a poet and novelist.
He is the author of *Unrelated Individuals
Forming a Group Waiting to Cross* (Penguin),
The Making of Collateral Beauty (Tupelo)
and *The Importance of Peeling Potatoes in
Ukraine* (Penguin). His most recent book is
an unconventional guide to
reading and writing poems: *Poetry:
A Survivor's Guide* (Bloomsbury).